COPLAND GERSHWIN BERNSTEIN

Celebrating American Diversity

For My Dear
Friend Lou,
Listen, Read and Enjoy!
Bob

by
Robert Moon

COPLAND, GERSHWIN & BERNSTEIN
Celebrating American Diversity

ISBN 978-0-9834370-7-9

Printed in the United States of America

Cover Design by Jeff Dunn

Published by:

Big Hat Press
Lafayette, California
www.bighatpress.com

CONTENTS

INTRODUCTION

Celebrating American Diversity

There used to be a time when classical musicians were a part of the main stage of America's creative artists and helped define who we were as Americans. It was a time when America was weaning itself from its dependency on European culture and struggling to define what was distinctly American. For decades American orchestral repertoire—and most recordings—were almost exclusively the domain of the great composers from the past—Haydn, Mozart, Beethoven, Schubert, Brahms—and all the others that had survived the test of time. Immigrants had flocked to America to start new lives but it wasn't until the mid-twentieth century that they had mingled and intermarried to create a new musical culture separate from their origins.

Copland, Gershwin and Bernstein all came from Russian Jewish cultures to settle in the melting pot that was New York City in the early twentieth century. Once in that environment, their personalities and family cultures took all three in different directions. Copland had to go to Europe to discover and integrate his musical training and emerge as an American classical composer. Gershwin's natural affinity for Broadway merged with lessons from a classical music teacher and knowledge of classical music. His musical brilliance and lack of formal musical training resulted in iconic works that brought Broadway to Carnegie Hall. Bernstein's multitalented personality—conductor, composer and teacher—made him the face of classical music in the mid twentieth century, but he's also remembered for writing the score of a great American Broadway musical, *West Side Story*.

Although they took different paths, all three assimilated, recognized and integrated America's diverse cultures into significant classical music that was distinctly American. No longer were American composers little more than clones of their famous European brethren. Moreover, they had the personalities to bring their music into mainstream American culture. Some will point to Ives and Toscanini as being major influences in classical music. But Toscanini brought the great European composers to Americans in exciting interpretations that utilized the media of his time. The subtext of Joseph Horowitz's book *Understanding Toscanini* said it best: "How He Became an American Culture-God and Helped to Create a New Audience for Old Music." Charles Ives did integrate his New England culture into music that was American, but few knew of his existence as a composer, and his music was too radical to break into the American popular idiom.

As the socio-political columnist David Brooks has pointed out in a *New York Times* editorial of June 28, 2013, America is a "nation of mutts." In 1960, 75% of the foreign-born population came from Europe, complete with European musical heritage. The percent of foreign-born residents has grown from 5% in 1960 to 13% today. Americans of European descent are already a minority among 5-year-olds. Look no further for the reason that classical music has an aging audience. The generation that funds American orchestras and other musical institutions, that buys tickets and CDs, grew up listening to the great composers, most of whom are European. That's why they still play the 'great' European composers as a staple of their musical diet. Copland, Gershwin and Bernstein were able to break through and add great American music to that European mix and put American music on their generation's radar. How they did that is the story of this book.

But today America is "a nation with hundreds of fluid ethnicities from around the world, intermarrying and intermingling. European-Americans will be a minority overall in 30 years at the latest, and probably sooner," Brooks asserts. Few will question the assumption that diversity is one characteristic that has made America a great nation. Today the world seems to be re-tribalizing rather than being able to integrate differences into a national synergy that fosters economic and social growth. Despite the political gridlock that chokes our national government, America has shown an amazing ability to integrate ethnic, social and racial differences compared to the rest of the world.

The classical music that's being written in America today has been adept at integrating past forms and styles with different cultural and popular traditions to create a new musical language that is creative, significantly complex, yet understandable. There is an explosion of music being written today that represents the new diversity of the American and world landscape. John Adams, Golijov, Reich, Gubaidulina, Bright Sheng, Sallinen, Muhly, and hundreds more are composing music that integrates their modern culture(s) with the giants of the past.

Today American composers revel in the clashing of cultures and the ability to network with each other to create new music that speaks to the increasing diversity of American culture. The question is whether American musical institutions will change fast enough to present this new music to new audiences fast enough to survive.

AARON COPLAND

Defining American Music

When Aaron Copland left for Paris in 1938, he took two collections of cowboy music with him. Although he didn't have to use them, "it wasn't very long before I found myself hopelessly involved in expanding, contracting, rearranging and superimposing cowboy tunes on the rue de Rennes in Paris," he wrote. He was commissioned to write the music to Eugene Loring's new ballet based on the story of the famous gunman and western outlaw, Billy the Kid. Later, in a 1976 interview in *Newsweek*, mentioning the myriad of books and films on the lore of the American West, he modestly added, "Every American has a feeling of what the West is like—you absorb it. It was just a feat of the imagination."

Some imagination! If there was ever music that shouted "This is the American West" it's *Billy the Kid*. The vistas of loneliness of the open prairie—the exuberant promise of a street in a frontier town, the joy of a Mexican dance—have entered the musical idiom of our cowboy heritage. The ephemeral beauty of a quiet moonlit night during a card game explodes into a violent and exciting gun battle. A rowdy celebration of Billy's capture and the bittersweet beauty of his death are reprised by a grand vision of life on the open prairie. It's a vivid and brilliantly colored musical reverie that presaged Hollywood's depiction of our romantic west. Copland followed it in 1942 with the score to Agnes de Mille's ballet *Rodeo*. A tomboy fails to compete with the riding skills of men, so she displays her feminine strengths and wins her man. There's a raucous party ("Buckaroo Holiday"), a touching "Corral Nocturne," a "Saturday Night Waltz" and a vivacious "Hoe Down" that matches the authenticity of its creator's personality.

Twenty-three years after his death in 1990, Aaron Copland's music is still part of America's culture. The background music to a recent commercial was a percussive, upbeat arrangement of the Shaker melody 'Simple gifts' that Copland made famous in his ballet *Appalachian Spring*. Drawing from the indigenous tunes of American folklore and its history, Copland composed a group of works that became synonymous with populist music in America. When asked why director Spike Lee used Copland's music in his 1998 basketball film, *He Got Game*, Lee answered, "When I hear Copland, I hear America, and basketball is American." The music Copland wrote in the 1930's unified and inspired our diverse population. How did a Jewish kid from Brooklyn—and gay to boot—emerge as one of the most beloved and recognized American musical voices?

Aaron Copland (1900-90) was raised in immigrant-rich Brooklyn, absorbing the sounds of burgeoning urban America while growing up in the same neighborhood and at the same time as George Gershwin. Although they were cut from different musical cloths, classical and Broadway, it's a tribute to the powerful influence of their milieu that two distinctly different and authentic American voices emerged from identical environments. Like Leonard Bernstein, Aaron had to persuade his family that music was his calling; to really fulfill his compositional gifts he followed his instincts and first went to Paris at age 21 to study with the legendary pedagogue Nadia Boulanger. Copland became Boulanger's star student, studied orchestration, score reading and analysis, and met Stravinsky, Ravel, Poulenc and many other composers and authors.

COPLAND THE POPULIST

Copland returned to America with a new perspective on his native land. "You become more sentimental in Paris about Brooklyn in a way that you could never be sentimental about Brooklyn while living there," he commented. But it wasn't until 1932 when he visited his friend, the Mexican composer Carlos Chávez, that he saw the possibilities of writing music connected to American history and folklore. He was mesmerized by the vivacious music found in a local Mexican dance hall and saw in the Mexican people a populism he admired. *El salon México* (1936), loosely based on Mexican folk themes, was the result of this inspiration. It abounds in color, is brilliantly impulsive and rhythmically exhilarating. It quickly became very popular and soon became a link to the music of the American West. Transplants from south of the border brought a vital musical vocabulary that enriched the musical "sound" that conveys the landscapes and people of the American West. Copland adopted this new melodic, rhythmic and harmonic palette that found full voice in his great ballet trilogy that defined what we think of as distinctly American.

Following *Billy the Kid* and *Rodeo*, in 1944 Copland turned to Pennsylvania Shaker lore in his music written for Martha Graham's ballet, *Appalachian Spring*. Originally titled "A Ballet for Martha," Copland said of the great dancer and choreographer, "...she's unquestionably very American: there's something prim and restrained, simple yet strong, about her that one tends to think of as American." In fact, although Copland thought her work to be "severe," obviously his description of her also fit the composer himself: both were major figures who reflected colloquial Americana in their respective art forms. When at a first rehearsal, Copland asked Graham, "What did you name the ballet? She answered, "*Appalachian Spring*." He asked, "Where did you get the name?" She replied, "From a poem by Hart Crane." "Does it have anything to do with the ballet," he asked? "No," she said, "I just liked the title and took it."

The story focuses on a young couple, the enthusiastic construction of their house, a warning from a revivalist preacher about "fate", an interlude of a "Day of Wrath" (reflective of World War II), and the glorious ending using the well-known Shaker hymn, "Tis the Gift to be Simple." *Appalachian Spring* is unique in American music—one of the few works beloved by both critics and audiences. But what are the elements of Copland's music that makes it American?

COPLAND AND THE AMERICAN SOUND

Copland used broad lyrical themes that represented monumental characteristics of the American landscape—towering mountains and vast prairies. He left expressive spaces between notes, giving air around chords that mimicked the expansive American terrain. Dissonances reflected the construction of our burgeoning urban landscape following World War I. Dance rhythms came courtesy of our neighbors to the south in Mexico and the rest of Latin America. He borrowed techniques used by jazz and popular dance bands of his time—syncopation (rhythmic accents falling on weak beats when strong beats are silent), polyrhythms (simultaneous use of strikingly different rhythms) and persistent repetition of melodic phrases (ostinato). Copland modified American folk tunes by changing accents and phrasing. Rapidly shifting moods created drama. His textures were clear, and he made a concerted effort to simplify his music, i.e. to say what he needed to say using the fewest notes possible. It was a distinctly American musical language, different from the complex, atonal and thickly orchestrated music that emanated from some Europeans in the early twentieth century.

FILM SCORES AND A GREAT AMERICAN SYMPHONY

Capitalizing on the popularity of *El Salon Mexico* (and to earn some extra money), Copland visited Hollywood in 1937. The movie industry had begun to use serious composers as a source for film scores—Korngold's *Anthony and Adverse* and George Antheil's *The Plainsman* were successful examples. However, his overtures to filmmakers were rejected because he had no experience in writing film music. But an opportunity arose to compose the score for a 45-minute documentary, *The City* (1939), whose purpose was to advocate "a progressive, humanistic and essentially socialist approach to city planning." The film became a classic and Copland's music perfectly fits the various urban scenarios depicted—"New England Countryside," "The Steel Mill," "Sunday Traffic," "Taxi Jam," "The Children," and "The New City"—among others. He went on to score many other films, and two won Academy Award nominations—*Of Mice and Men* and *North Star*. Copland's film scores, like his populist masterpieces, provided a model of how to depict the diverse American landscape in cinema. Copland biographer Howard Pollock includes Jerome Moross' score for *The Big Country* and Elmer Bernstein's *The Magnificient Seven* as examples of Copland's cinematic influence.

Using the money earned from the film score *North Star*, Copland started work on his Third Symphony. The lengthy (over 40 minutes) four-movement work is grand in conception and contains the best of the composer's orchestral powers. Copland's use of his *Fanfare for the Common Man* in the final movement never fails to bring a tear to my eye. At the end of Bernstein's 1958 "Young Peoples Concert" program on "What Makes Music American," he introduces Aaron Copland as the "Dean of American Music," enthusiastically pronouncing that his Symphony No. 3 contains "jazz rhythms, and wide open optimism, and wide open spaces, and the simplicity, and the sentimentality, and a mixture of things from all over the world, a noble fanfare, a hymn, everything." Copland then conducted the finale of the Third Symphony. Author Clifford Odets wrote Copland, calling it "one of the most moving experiences I've had in years." Maybe it's the honesty and dignity in the symphony that connects with audiences. Certainly it deserves consideration as one of the greatest American symphonies ever written.

As a response to Pearl Harbor, conductor Andre Kostelanetz commissioned Copland and two other composers (Virgil Thompson and Jerome Kern) to write musical depictions of famous Americans. The moving *Lincoln Portrait* (1942) for narrator and orchestra has offered many opportunities for actors and politicians to associate themselves with this sometimes excessively patriotic tone poem—from Adlai Stevenson, Charlton Heston, Paul Newman, Katharine Hepburn—to Barack Obama. My experience of a terminally ill well-known San Francisco columnist Herb Caen's recitation (with the San Francisco Symphony) remains an affecting memory.

The Clarinet Concerto (1947-8), commissioned by Benny Goodman, was written on a South American tour sponsored by the U.S. State Department. It contains some musical references to South American sounds, a favorite of Copland since his 1932 visit to Mexico that produced *El Salon Mexico*. Goodman expressed doubts about being able to perform it, and it wasn't until 1950 that he introduced it. The first movement contains yearning, lyrical music, some of Copland's most beautiful. The remainder is peppered with jazz elements and a Brazilian tune.

In 1952 Copland received a grant from the League of Composers to write an opera for television, *The Tender Land*, (1952-4) based on James Agee's book, *Let Us Now Praise Famous Men* and the Depression-era photographs of Walker Evans. It tells the story of two strangers who come upon a Midwestern farm family. The young daughter Laurie falls in love with Martin, but the romance is terminated when the interlopers leave. Copland made a suite of the music, and the aria, "The Promise of Living," sung by five of the principals, is one of Copland's most appealing moments. Although the networks weren't interested in broadcasting it, the New York City Opera gave the premiere in 1954.

While many of Copland's populist compositions address external events, *Twelve Poems of Emily Dickinson* (1950-2) reveals the introverted and quiet side of his personality. The first two songs depict mildly contrasting views of nature—the comforting "Nature, the Gentlest Mother" and the benign scare of a summer thunderstorm "There Came a Wind Like a Bugle." Two contrasting views of death follow—a spirited mockery, "Going to Heaven"—and a matter-of-fact acceptance, "The Chariot." I can't think of a more delightful set of American folk songs than the two sets *Old American Songs* (1950-55). The ten songs include two minstrel songs, two ballads, a revivalist song and "Simple Gifts" from *Appalachian Spring*. They touch the heart and soul of American folklore.

COPLAND THE MODERNIST

Although primarily known for his popular and tonal compositions, at the beginning and end of his life Copland was influenced by the revolution of atonal modernism that swept Europe in the early twentieth century. Many other North and South American composers went to Paris in the 1920's to learn from the European musical ferment centered there—Virgil Thompson, Roger Sessions, Walter Piston, Carlos Chávez, and others. As Copland commented in his *Music in the 20's* Public Television series, these young composers actually congregated in Paris for the ironic reason to break away from the "creative apron strings of European art" so that they could return to their mother county and write music reflecting their own nationalistic roots. Before Copland left Nadia Boulanger and Paris in 1921, she introduced him to conductor Serge Koussevitzky (Boston Symphony), who then commissioned Copland's first major work, *Organ Symphony* (1924). The radical nature of the new work shocked the audience when Walter Damrosch conducted it in New York City's Lewisohn Stadium. After the performance the Maestro quipped, "If a young man at the age of 25 can write a symphony like that, in five years he will be ready to commit murder!" It contains a quiet, pensive prelude, a jazzy scherzo, modern but tonal harmonies, and a powerful finale, complete with spiky rhythms and dissonances reminiscent of Stravinsky. It's an exciting and bold work that announced Copland as a major composer.

It was the beginning of Copland's "modernist period" in which he integrated what he learned in Paris with his American roots. Koussevitzky commissioned *Music for Theater* in 1925, a work inspired by the use of jazz by European composers (Stravinsky, Poulenc and Ravel). Copland defines jazz in *Music of the 20's* as expressive of American culture of the 1920's and "it had musical interest for composers." He names the characteristics of jazz in that 1965 video as "polyrhythmic structures, melodic turns of phrase, riffs, blue notes and breaks." But there's no mention of Gershwin as the first to use jazz in classical compositions, although he does mention *Rhapsody in Blue*. Nevertheless, *Music for Theater* expressed the boundless optimism of a growing urban culture through the use of daring dissonances, cross rhythms, muted trumpets, and sad, melodic refrains.

Copland's use of jazz in his Piano Concerto shocked many classical audiences and critics. "If there exists anywhere in the world a stranger concatenation of meaninglessly ugly sounds and distorted rhythms than Mr. Copland's Piano Concerto, Boston has been spared it," wrote Warren Storey Smith in the *Boston Post* of January 27, 1927. Written a year after Gershwin's Concerto in F, Copland's Piano Concerto is more introspective, raucous, sardonic, but lots of fun.

As his modernist works gained respect among other American

composers in the late 1920's and early 1930's, Copland emerged as the leader of the American avant garde. Along with Roger Sessions he organized concerts of new American music and helped composers publish their scores. His music continued to break new ground long before he entered his populist phase. The *Symphonic Ode* (1929) uses a huge orchestra to create impressively massive blocks of sound, balanced by brief but potent moments of Romanticism's highly valued *Sehnsucht*, the German term for longing or yearning. Copland thought the *Ode* one of his better works, but it has received few performances. The *Piano Variations* (1931), orchestrated in 1957 as the *Orchestral Variations*, is one of Copland's more innovated and respected works. Its rhythmic complexity and blazing orchestration grabs the listener's attention and never surrenders its grip. It is not a happy work, but America in the early 1930s was deep in the mire of the Great Depression.

The *Short Symphony* (No. 2) (1933) is transitional between his modernist and populist periods. Constant rhythmic changes and piano-punctuated dissonances are modern devices that lie beneath the overtly playful emotional tone of the first movement. Copland almost called the work "The Bounding Line." The melancholic middle movement becomes a plaintive song composed more than a decade before *Appalachian Spring*. The late program annotator and critic Michael Steinberg called it "a synthesis of the learned and the vernacular, thus, in all brevity [15 minutes], a singularly 'complete' representation of its composer."

By the early 1930's, America's Great Depression had intervened in Copland's life, and, although he survived by teaching contemporary music at the New School in New York City, his works weren't being played because they were deemed too large and too expensive, difficult for musicians to perform, and too radical for audiences. Concurrently, he met Frank Lloyd Wright, Martha Graham and others at the New School and became immersed in the artistic expressions of social unrest and the plight of the working class, devastated by the Depression. The works that emerged invoked pride in America's past, and encouraged art that portrayed the ideals of American nationalism. Copland began to look for something new, something connected to his American roots, and his populist period followed in 1938 with *Billy the Kid*.

LATE WORKS, CONDUCTOR AND EDUCATOR

By 1950, atonality (often called serialism or twelve-tone composition) had become the trend for American composers, and Copland wrestled with compositions using these techniques. In 1961 he was invited to write a work for the New York Philharmonic that would be featured at the opening of Lincoln Center's Philharmonic Hall. The concert was broadcast on television. Instead of writing something celebratory, he decided to compose a work that would reflect the "tensions, aspirations and drama inherent in the world of today" in a modern, dissonant style. *Connotations for Orchestra* shocked an audience that expected a melodic work in the populist vein. Mrs. John F. Kennedy exclaimed, "Oh, Mr. Copland, Oh, Mr. Copland..." Few, including most critics, liked the piece, not wanting to be reminded of the reality of an unfriendly urban world. Even for one who warms to atonality, it's a difficult work—almost unremittingly bleak. *Inscape* (1967) is quieter, leaner but cut from the same dissonant cloth.

Aaron Copland, 1960
Credit: Library of Congress

Sometimes a composer's personality is best revealed in rehearsal, where he can be more forthright and intimate with fellow musicians. In a 1973 rehearsal of a recording of *Appalachian Spring* with the Columbia Chamber Ensemble, Copland starts by saying, "I assume you know the work" and an orchestra member replies, "Only by reputation." After some chuckles by the others, the maestro says, "A warm sound, warm, without any effort, and sort of a noncommittal clarinet sound" and the orchestra begins the rehearsal. Yet later, he implores the orchestra: "This is a barn dance, get in the mood!" He got what he wanted, but was civil about it most of the time. He was a self-taught conductor, and his mentor Leonard Bernstein was more than pleased to teach him. His major conducting career started in the early 1950's and lasted until the late 1970's, conducting his own music and that of many established contemporary composers. He recorded many of his own works on several records with the London Symphony Orchestra. His interpretations, although obviously authentic, were straightforward, but not without energy and compassion. They are a contrast to the sometimes indulgently expressive Bernstein, a testament to how differing interpretations reveal different facets of great music.

Although he collaborated with Vivian Perlis on two autobiographical volumes, his 1965 televised lectures on "Music in the 20's" are a succinct historical summary of one of classical music's revolutionary periods, and also provide an intimate window into Copland's straightforward and introverted personality. He was generous in choosing his colleagues to demonstrate musical examples: Paul Jacobs, Lotte Lenya, the Juilliard Quartet, David Tudor, Igor Stravinsky and, of course, himself. There's a wonderful performance of Hindemith's hilarious operatic sketch, *Hin und Zuruck* (*There and Back*) with Beverly Sills, conducted by Sarah Caldwell. The twelve half-hour segments included: Jazz and Jazz Influence; American Music in the 20's; Central Europe: 12-Tone Revolution; New Movements in Opera and Neo-Classicism and others. Copland doesn't have the pizzazz of Bernstein and the black and white video lacks the movement of today's fast-paced editing, but what emerges are knowledgeable, concise and authentic presentations from someone who was a participant in the history he's summarizing.

By the mid-1970's Copland began to lose his memory and gradually cut back on his public appearances, sustained by a revolving number of housekeepers, mostly musicians or composers, at his Rock Hill home in the lower Hudson Valley in New York. He died in 1990, only two months after Leonard Bernstein's passing. The Copland Collection is now housed in the Library of Congress, and the Aaron Copland House in Cortlandt Manor, New York is a National Historical Landmark. It houses a composer-in-residence program, and is open to the public by appointment.

Perhaps the most notable tribute to Copland's lasting greatness is the large number of his works that have become part of the standard symphonic repertory, including ballet scores. He was the first to prove that a composer in America can make a living from his music rather than being tethered to academia. Of the man, his friend Mina Lederman Daniel said, "There was always a modesty about him...there is still in him a modicum of wonder about it all." Leonard Bernstein summed it up when he said, "He's the best we have, you know." As the 2012 presidential election has shown, racial, economic, ethnic and age differences still divide our country. When I listen to Copland's music, I'm moved by the images of an America that is a part of a common history that binds us together. That's his gift to us, and why we need his music more than ever today.

George Gershwin at the piano in his New York
City apartment, circa 1934

Credit: Ira and Leonore Gershwin Trusts

GEORGE GERSHWIN

Jazz and Musical Theater Come to Carnegie Hall

MIXING AMERICA'S MUSICAL ROOTS

If Aaron Copland created classical music's "American Sound," George Gershwin (1898-1937) brought the popular American music of his time into the classical concert hall. Today, composers move easily between multiple musical styles, but in the early twentieth century there was great resistance to combining genres, because ethnic divisions in the America of that day claimed proprietary rights to "their" music. Born in Brooklyn, Gershwin was a second generation Russian Jew and musical theater was his domain. African-Americans rightfully claimed ownership of jazz. And the primary performers and funders of classical music were Anglo-Saxon whites (mostly males) and Russian European Jews. When Gershwin used jazz in his scores, there were protests from African-Americans, while those in the classical camp criticized his forays into "their" genre because he lacked formal European classical training. Copland had to go to Europe and be exposed to Stravinsky, Poulenc and Ravel before he deemed jazz "appropriate" to use in his own compositions.

But a closer look at Gershwin's music reveals that its genesis comes from the kind of blended diversity that has been the foundation for American popular culture and artistic life. His musical roots are tangled up with a range of influences, from the Yiddish theater of early 20th century New York, to vaudeville, ragtime (of Scott Joplin and others), Latin American (Cuban) music, and Irving Berlin and Jerome Kern's Tin Pan Alley hits. All these influences can be found in his music, along with the Anglo-American art songs of the 1890's and the post-Romantic, Impressionistic music of Ravel, Stravinsky, Schoenberg and Prokofiev.

Born in Brooklyn and raised in Manhattan, two years before and only blocks from Aaron Copland, George Gershwin was brought up in a middle class family, which included his older brother and eventual collaborator, Ira. Young George showed little interest in school, preferring to play street hockey. But in 1910 his family bought a piano. His attraction to it was immediate, and at 15 he was performing at summer resorts in the Catskill Mountains. Before recordings, there was sheet music and pianos in homes: George became a song-plugger at Remicks, a publisher of popular music in Tin Pan Alley. Doing so gave him valuable experience at keyboard improvisation and transposing. But he also showed an interest in traditional classical music, taking lessons from a classical music teacher.

Gershwin, however, was Broadway bound, and began his career as one of the great composers of the American musical theater, starting with New York City review called *DemiTasse*, which contained a number that was a parody of Stephen Foster's song "Old Folks at Home" called "Swanee." When Gershwin played it at a party, Al Jolson heard it and incorporated it into his own show, *Sinbad*. Jolson recorded it in 1920 and it became a hit. Eventually George's brother Ira joined him as lyricist.

RHAPSODY IN BLUE

On January 4, 1924, while playing pool, Ira handed George an article in the *New York Tribune* that pronounced that George was composing and performing a "jazz piano concerto" to be premiered with bandleader Paul Whiteman's Palais Royal Orchestra at one of the temples of classical music, Aeolian Hall, on February 12. Whiteman had labeled the concert "An Experiment in Modern Music" and later invited classical critics and several renowned musicians—composer/pianist Sergei Rachmaninoff, violinist Jascha Heifetz, among others. Gershwin was shocked! He had talked about writing a jazz work for Whiteman in late 1923, but had not committed to the project. The article, it turned out, was a publicity stunt by Whiteman, who wanted to upstage a competitor. The gambit worked: four days later, Gershwin started composing *Rhapsody in Blue*, finishing the jazz band version in three weeks. With no time to fully orchestrate it, the task fell to Ferde Grofé, who only a few years later achieved fame as the composer of the popular *Grand Canyon Suite.* Ira suggested the name, *Rhapsody in Blue*, inspired by an exhibit by the American painter James McNeill Whistler, who titled some of his paintings after colors. Upon hearing the sultry clarinet glissando that launches the work, the audience was startled. The reviewer for the *New York Sun* "ached to dance up and down the aisles." Henry O. Osgood, in his book, *So This is Jazz*, called it the first work "that allowed jazz to stick its head outside the cabaret door." Gershwin became famous overnight. Although Whiteman lost $7,000 on the concert, he made up for the loss in repeat performances. He later commissioned works from Copland, Duke Ellington and Grofé.

TIN PAN ALLEY INVADES CARNEGIE HALL

Rhapsody in Blue brought jazz into the concert hall, but it wasn't the ragtime, blues, and spirituals heard at black nightclubs. Nor was it the rarified nature of jazz that Stravinsky, Milhaud, Copland and others used in their classical compositions. It was jazz in the American popular tradition—acceptable to white audiences played by white musicians. The shock of discovery experienced by those first audiences may have lost its power today because of the curse of excessive familiarity, but the verve and spirit of *Rhapsody in Blue* still remains.

Walter Damrosch, conductor of the New York Symphony, was in the audience at the premiere of *Rhapsody in Blue*, and he was so impressed that a few months later he commissioned Gershwin to compose a piano concerto, with the composer as soloist. Even though he originally called it *New York Concerto*, he changed the name to Concerto in F, proving to the classical world that he could compose a piece of "absolute music." Gershwin had taken lessons from Rubin Goldmark and Henry Cowell, and said that he "went out to buy a book on musical form to find out how a concerto was constructed." Recent biographer Howard Pollock claims that comment was "more tongue in cheek," and Cowell described Gershwin as a student: "His fertile mind leaped all over the place. He was exasperated at the rules—but not because he was incapable of mastering them. With no effort at all he rattled off almost perfect exercises, but would get sidetracked into something—using a juicy ninth and altered chords that he liked better..."

And Gershwin's own description of the Concerto in F reveals a musician more interested in the work's content and energies than its allegiance to any particular style. "The first section employs the Charleston rhythm. It is quick and pulsating, representing the young enthusiastic spirit of American life. The second movement conveys a poetic, nocturnal tone courtesy of a slow and wistful trumpet solo. It utilizes the atmosphere of what has come to be referred to as the American blues...The final movement is an orgy of rhythm, starting violently and keeping to the same pace throughout." Concerto in F shows a deft use of "classical" techniques—repetition and development of melodic motifs, juxtaposition of jazz and classical material, rhythmic vitality and key shifts. Still, Gershwin's restless musical spirit was never harnessed by formal classical strictures.

Concerto in F premiered on December 3, 1925, and received a favorable critical response. Damrosch wrote, "Various composers have been walking around jazz like a cat around a plate of hot soup, waiting for it to cool off, so they could enjoy it without burning their tongues, hitherto accustomed only to the more tepid liquid distilled by cooks of the classical school." He went on to anoint Gershwin as "the prince who has taken Cinderella by the hand and openly proclaimed her a princess to the astonished world, no doubt to the fury of her envious sisters." Prokofiev considered it nothing more than a succession of 32-bar Broadway style tunes. But the overall critical response was positive and Gershwin performed it often in his lifetime.

It's the most-played piano concerto by an American composer, and it integrates jazz and classical idioms with brilliance, verve and *joie de vivre*. In the 1951 film *An American in Paris* Oscar Levant plays a cut version of the last movement of the Concerto in F—in a dream fantasy that has him doing more than double-duty as the conductor and the musicians. It's a hoot!

PARIS AND HOLLYWOOD

Along with *Rhapsody in Blue* and Concerto in F, the three Piano Preludes completed a classical trilogy that Gershwin completed between 1925 and 1926. In ABA, or "song" pattern, the three sections of the Piano Preludes are balanced with a slow middle movement sandwiched between two outer sections. Each short movement is melodically distinct and harmonically matched with its thematic material. It's a perfectly balanced gem, reflective and playful.

George Gerswhin, 1927

In 1928 Gershwin went to Europe and visited Maurice Ravel, Darius Milhaud, Francis Poulenc, Alban Berg and William Walton. Ravel declined to give him composition lessons, but Berg spoke warmly of his music and Walton "was hypnotized by his fabulous piano-playing and melodic gift." This trip inspired him to write the rhapsodic *An American in Paris*, which was premiered on December 13, 1928, Walter Damrosch conducting. The new work was the composer's love letter to Paris. Howard Pollock's biography quotes Gershwin's description: "This piece describes an American's visit to the gay and beautiful city of Paris. We see him sauntering down the Champs Elysées walking stick in hand, tilted straw hat, drinking in sights, and other things as well. We see the effects of French wine, which makes him homesick for America. And that's where the blue begins. I mean the blues begin. He finally emerges from his stupor to realize once again that he is in the gay city of Paree, listening to taxi horns, the noise of the boulevards, and the music of the can-can, and thinking, 'Home is swell! But after all, this is Paris—so let's go!'" Poulenc called it one of the great works of the twentieth century, and most critics admired the work's élan and energy. It's hard not to smile when hearing Gershwin's use of the Parisian taxi horns, which he brought back from Paris. Vincent Minnelli's 1951 movie *An American in Paris* features a visually stunning if musically altered 17-minute fantasy-ballet that captures Gershwin's exhilaration with the "City of Light."

Gershwin ventured to Hollywood in 1930, hoping to compose for the silver screen and take advantage of the advent of "talking films" in 1927. But "Delicious," the musical comedy he scored, was a flop. However, the dream sequence in the film, titled "New York Rhapsody" (sharply cut in the movie), became the genesis of his *Second Rhapsody for Orchestra with Piano*, premiered in 1932 by Serge Koussevitsky and the Boston Symphony Orchestra. Inevitably it was compared, and not favorably, to *Rhapsody in Blue*, but this work was more ambitious as a classical work. Koussevitsky remarked, "I was amazed at his talent...It is a masterful orchestration. Finished—complete. It is not jazz, it is symphonic—a new development that has come from jazz. Very interesting, the boy's talent does not stop with composition—his talent to orchestrate is what amazes me." Most critics recognized its greater sophistication, but "at the cost of earlier and irresistible élan."

George Gershwin at the piano in his New York City apartment, circa 1934
Credit: Ira and Leonore Gershwin Trusts

As happened in the case of Copland's *El Salon Mexico*, Gershwin's *Cuban Overture* was inspired by a vacation in Cuba. For Gershwin, it was the nightclub serenade of a sixteen-piece band that led to his *Overture* with its use of bongos, maracas, gourds and "Cuban sticks."

Gershwin had conquered Broadway, enjoyed his classical successes, but his brief, unsuccessful flirtation with Hollywood had left him looking for new vistas to conquer. He found them in his opera *Porgy and Bess*.

PORGY AND BESS

Why did a nice Jewish boy from New York choose a novel written by a southern white gentleman about a black beggar living in a Charleston, South Carolina tenement, as the subject for his second opera? Gershwin's love of jazz led him to explore African-American spirituals, and he developed an affinity for black culture and lifestyle. The "drama, the humor, the superstition, the religious fervor, the dancing and irrepressible high spirits of the race," Gershwin said, drew him to their music.

Gershwin's interest in writing an American opera can be traced to 1921 when he wrote a short "jazz opera" based in Harlem, *Blue Monday Blues*. In 1926 he read and was smitten by *Porgy*, a novel by Edwin DuBose Heyward, based on the real life of a man named Goat Sammy. Taken with the novel, Gershwin contacted the author.

But DuBose's wife had already turned the novel into a very successful Broadway stage play—it had an impressive 367 performances. So the project was stalled and Gershwin busied himself with major hits in both the classical and Broadway realms. Finally, in 1932, Heyward and Gershwin signed a contract for setting the story to music. To immerse himself in the context, Gershwin worked in author Heyward's Folly Island shack for over a month to absorb the Gullah population's culture and music, the setting for *Porgy and Bess*. Walter Rimler's book, *George Gershwin—An Intimate Portrait* contains a colorful exposition of Gershwin's experience.

Gershwin wanted something more than a musical, but did not want it to be limited to a mere handful of performances as an opera. He called it a "folk opera." Heyward wrote the libretto and co-authored the lyrics with Ira Gershwin. Gullah dialect was used for the sung recitatives and some of the music came from spirituals. Some critics have compared the choruses in *Porgy and Bess* to those in Wagner's *Die Meistersinger von Nürnberg* and the big arias to Bizet's *Carmen*.

Porgy and Bess demonstrates Gershwin's ability to write music of ravishing beauty that expresses the emotional trajectory of the characters throughout the arc of the drama. Not just the 'big' numbers, e.g., "Summertime," "Oh, I got plenty o' nuttin', an' nuttin's plenty fo'me," "Bess, you is my woman now," "It ain't necessarily so," but also Porgy's "Buzzard Song" with chorus in Act 2, the strong drum introduction to Act II, Scene 2 and the fresh and brief aria "Strawberry Woman," in Act II, Scene 3. The hurricane sextet and the orchestral accompaniment are somewhat reminiscent of Debussy, with "scene painting" in the orchestration to bring the storm to life. The flaws that critics have pointed out have centered on the work's length and structural transitions. Various versions have been tinkered with over the years to a range of reactions.

The audience at the New York opening on October 10, 1935 cheered loudly at the conclusion. Many were left in tears and the large party afterward was one of the great moments in Gershwin's life. Critical reaction was mixed, hardly surprising for one of the first operatic-musical hybrids. Theater and drama critics' reactions ranged from Arthur Pollock's comment in the *Brooklyn Daily Eagle* that "This is the sort of thing that Pulitzer Prizes are not good enough for" to Paul Rosenfeld's comment that it was "an aggrandized musical show." The classical critic Virgil Thompson said that "Gershwin doesn't know what an opera is" but also said "and yet *Porgy and Bess* is an opera and it has power and vigor." Biographer Pollock makes the point that "whatever their reservations, the great majority of both drama and music critics loved the piece, which they widely deemed not only Gershwin's finest achievement to date but the best American opera ever written, and a milestone in the development of a national opera." Alex Ross comments that "*Porgy* performed the monumental feat of reconciling the rigidity of Western notated music with the African-American principle of improvised variation."

A SUDDEN FINALE

Like many men, Gershwin was so busy with his projects that he said little to his friends about the loss of energy and headaches that started to occur by May of 1937. Rimler's biography details his final days. Complaining often about his health convinced Ira and his domineering wife Lenore that George's concerns were the expressions of a hypochondriac. There were times when his ills receded, as when Aaron Copland visited Gershwin, asking him to sign an application for his membership into the American Society of Composers, Authors and Publishers, so Copland could write film scores. When leaving the Brown Derby after lunch with Ira and Leonore, George fell to the sidewalk. Leonore callously said, "Leave him there, all he wants is attention." A visit to the Cedars of Lebanon Hospital garnered the opinions that the problem was emotional, except for one doctor who suspected a brain tumor, but Gershwin refused a spinal tap. On the evening of July 9, he collapsed in a coma, and after a five-hour operation, George Gershwin died. Writer John O'Hara expressed the world's shock by saying, "George died on July 11, 1937, but I don't have to believe it if I don't want to."

Gershwin's attraction to popular and classical music was a product of his environment, and the excellence of his body of work in both genres is his lasting gift to the world. He was able to create music that was loved and respected by both sophisticated musical minds and the unpretentious listener. His music's melodic and emotional generosity, vibrant rhythms, thrilling climaxes and brilliant colors were an expression of his passionate personality. His work captured the spirit of an age; people were moved and uplifted by his music; his music influenced both classical and popular composers too numerous to mention. But the biggest proof that he's one of America's great composers is that his music is played today—and often!

LEONARD BERNSTEIN

AMERICA'S CLASSICAL MUSIC EVANGELIST

LARGER THAN LIFE

When the Bernstein household wheeled in a sad looking, brown upright piano that Aunt Clara wanted to get rid of, ten-year-old Leonard recalled, "And I remember *touching* it....and that was it. That was my contract with life, with God. From then on....I had found my universe, my place where I felt safe. This thing suddenly made me feel supreme..." And America had found the native-born musician, author, teacher, composer, writer, pianist and conductor who personified the democratization of classical music for the next five generations.

The first time I heard Leonard Bernstein was at a concert in Hill Auditorium in Ann Arbor, Michigan on September 12, 1967, when the New York Philharmonic visited the University of Michigan and Lenny conducted Mahler's Fourth Symphony and Ives' Second Symphony. There he was, his body flailing over the podium like an electronic octopus, conducting my new compositional heartthrob,

Mahler, and the eclectic American Ives' tribute to his early life in New England. As a conductor, Bernstein was in the process of making those two compositional giants familiar to anyone interested in classical music, through recordings, live concerts and his inimitable passionate persona captured through the new medium of television.

It was the enthusiasm and vitality that flowed out of his body like a lawn sprinkler on a hot day that made him a theatrical presence that changed the way America related to music. He took Gershwin's dual talents in classical and theatrical music to a new level, composing America's greatest "Broadway opera," *West Side Story*, the music for Elia Kazan's movie, *On the Waterfront*, and Jerome Robbins' ballet *Fancy Free*. At the same time, he wrote and presented television programs on such diverse subjects as "Introduction to Modern Music," "Jazz in the Concert Hall," and "What Makes Music Symphonic." He championed and performed American composers—Copland, Schuman, Ives, Harris and others. Whether it was the Beatles or Beethoven, Leonard Bernstein (1918-1990) had the knack of ardently explaining why and how music was an essential part of being alive.

A man with so much passion and energy was bound to influence more than America's musical life. With his Jewish background and the early years of living in the radical political-cultural era of government-sponsored Depression arts, he merged music with politics in his senior year at Harvard in 1939 by mounting a performance of his friend Marc Blitzstein's pro-union opera, *The Cradle Will Rock*. In 1947, along with 50 Hollywood and New York artists, Bernstein signed a manifesto condemning the House Un-American Activities Committee for blacklisting artists. When the State Department denied his application for a passport renewal in 1953, suspecting him of Communist ties, Bernstein had to spend $3500 in legal fees to get it back. His retort: "That's what it costs today to be a free American." His wife Felicia's 1970 meeting in their apartment to raise legal funds for the American Civil Liberties Union's defense of the thirteen Black Panthers being held in prison was infamously memorialized in Tom Wolfe's harsh New York magazine article, "Radical Chic."

Like Mahler, his musical soul mate, he was constantly torn between conducting—which satisfied his need to be at the center of the classical music world—and a desperate need to be recognized as a serious composer. He loved the adulation that conducting brought him, but couldn't stand the isolation that composition demanded. His physical presence and flamboyant energy screamed eroticism, but he couldn't reconcile his need for traditional family surroundings and his sexual preference for men. He lived in a time of avant garde domination of classical music, but never could stray from his love for tonality.

Leonard Bernstein with wife Felicia and children
Credit: Library of Congress

CHOOSING TO CONDUCT

Bernstein's father, Sam, had fled Russia with millions of other Jews and settled in New York City, later moving to Boston. When Bernstein first discovered the piano at age 10, playing it became a myopic focus of his early years, despite his father's resistance to a musical career for his son. At thirteen, he performed the first movement of the Grieg Piano Concerto at his temple. However, he was 16 before he went to his first symphony concert. His musical influences were as catholic as America in the 1930's—Klezmer and Cantorial music, the Broadway of Kern and Gershwin, jazz, and popular songs.

At Harvard, Bernstein was bored by academic theory classes and was known for his piano playing in different venues—jazz and the classics in college common rooms and waltzes at dance parties. He loved to play Copland's difficult *Piano Variations* as a demonstration of his pianistic brilliance. "I could empty a room, guaranteed, in two minutes," he boasted. In 1937 he met the mercurial conductor Dmitri Mitropoulos, whose mutual physical and intellectual attraction opened the door to the possibility of conducting as a career. He befriended Aaron Copland, who gave him feedback on his compositions and introduced him to America's leading composers and musicians. Gershwin provided him with a model of composer as performer, and Bernstein was devastated by his sudden death in 1937. After a year studying with a strict Fritz Reiner at the Curtis Institute, he met Serge Koussevitzky, the temperamental conductor of the Boston Symphony. As with Copland, and Mitropoulos, there ensued a frisson between Koussevitzky and Bernstein that merged the professional with the erotic. Bernstein was young, beautiful and a brilliant student. When Koussevitzky accepted him as one of five students in his master class at the newly-established Music Center at Tanglewood, the die was cast, and Bernstein knew he was going to be a conductor.

Koussevitsky convinced a reluctant Artur Rodzinsky to name Bernstein Assistant Conductor of the New York Philharmonic. "I have gone through all the conductors I know of in my mind," Rodzinsky said, "and I finally asked God whom I should take, and God said, 'Take Bernstein.'" That led to Bernstein's famous big break, the last-minute replacement of an ailing Bruno Walter on November 14, 1943, as conductor of a subscription program. "Here were players in their fifties and sixties with long experience. And this little snot-nose comes in and creates a more exciting performance. The orchestra stood up and cheered," violinist Jacques Margolies remembered. The concert was nationally broadcast, and the rest of the world discovered Leonard Bernstein, the conductor.

At age 25, he became a prominent man-about-town figure in New York City. Tallulah Bankhead famously commented after watching him conduct a rehearsal at Tanglewood, "Darling, I have gone mad over your back muscles. You must come and have dinner with me." He conducted, without pay but with much critical acclaim, the New York City Symphony for three years, and became the first American to conduct at La Scala (with Maria Callas, no less). He guest conducted the Boston Symphony and the New York Philharmonic. In 1951, he gave the American premiere of revolutionary composer Charles Ives' Second Symphony. Ives, then 71, refused to attend, but, listening to the performance on the radio at a friend's house, "danced a little jig." Finally, in 1958, he replaced Dmitri Mitropoulos as conductor of the New York Philharmonic. The Orchestra had stagnated, audiences declined, and the advent of stereo and the new medium of television gave the maestro an opportunity to launch one of the greatest periods in America's classical music history.

MAHLER'S SOUL MATE

Bernstein's eleven-year reign as Director of the New York Philharmonic (1958-69) breathed new life into the orchestra, changed the popular conception of classical music through his television programs, and earned money for the musicians through a spate of recordings using the new medium of stereo records. He was a part of a golden age of classical music in America—the late 50's through the 1970s—that witnessed the construction of new concert halls (Lincoln Center and many others); the expansion of symphony orchestras as a result of Ford Foundation grants; the establishment of a new federal agency, the National Endowment for the Arts; and the presence of great conductors in major American orchestras (Szell in Cleveland, Ormandy in Philadelphia, Munch in Boston, Reiner and Solti in Chicago, and Bernstein in New York).

When Bernstein arrived in 1958 he received additional responsibilities that consolidated his role as music leader of the orchestra: planning programs, organizing concert series, and selecting guest conductors and soloists. He established the Thursday evening concerts as "Previews" (where the orchestra wore Nehru jackets), spoke before performances, and initiated thematic programming, e.g., "Schumann and the Romantic Movement," "Keys to the Twentieth Century," and an overview of American music. He expanded his early televised *Omnibus* programs by presenting 53 "Young Peoples Concerts" in 14 years, even after he left the Philharmonic. He played the avant garde composers of his day—Elliott Carter, Milton Babbitt, Karlheinz Stockhausen—but only on one program, as he never embraced twelve-tone music. He often featured the tonal American music he loved—Aaron Copland, Roy Harris, William Schuman and others. His passionate advocacy of the American Charles Ives and Denmark's Carl Nielsen introduced their music to many Americans

But more than any other conductor, Leonard Bernstein greatly enhanced the reputation and enormous popularity of Gustav

Mahler's music through live performances, groundbreaking recordings and a widely-read and quoted article in *High Fidelity* magazine, "Mahler, His Time Has Come." It wasn't that Mahler was unknown to the New York Philharmonic; they had performed Mahler many times before 1958. But the emotional chemistry between Mahler's music and Bernstein's personality created a combustion that put the Austrian composer's symphonies on the world's musical map. "His music is so close to my heart—I feel attuned to it—a melancholy. An innocence. An attempt to recover life as it used to be—so untouched, so fresh. I understand his complexity, I love even his weaknesses, even if some of them are perhaps my own," he commented. In his "Who is Gustav Mahler?" Young Peoples Concert, Bernstein identifies himself with Mahler's problem—reconciling the conflict between composer and conductor.

He left the Philharmonic in 1969, taking his boundless energy to the conservative Vienna Philharmonic. In his later concerts and recording sessions with the Vienna, he "invented" Mahler for them by cajoling them to recognize and passionately perform a composer never acknowledged by their own countrymen as significant. Bernstein recognized the anti-Semitic bias that still pervaded musical Vienna far beyond Mahler's tenure with the Vienna Opera. Mahler, a Jew, converted to Catholicism a few months before his appointment to that post in 1897, partially as a way to secure the position. When Bernstein first went to Vienna to conduct the Vienna Philharmonic, he commented to American composer David Diamond, "I'm going to go to Vienna and teach those fucking Nazis how to play that Jew Mahler."

As it turned out, both conductor and musicians began a decade-long love affair between two opposites. Their recordings were bathed in far better sound but as he aged some of his interpretations sagged, at times distorted by mannered and exaggerated tempos. The best of those recordings include his Mozart symphonies, some Mahler, e.g., the *Sixth Symphony*, and Sibelius' *Seventh Symphony*. His favorite recordings were the Shostakovich *Seventh Symphony* with the Chicago Symphony Orchestra and the orchestral transcription of Beethoven's *String Quartet, Op. 131* with the Vienna Philharmonic. Bernstein was an education for the Viennese, but no more than his informative forays into American television.

THE GREAT COMMUNICATOR

If one had to use one word to describe Bernstein's genius, it would be *communicator*. When an unquenchable love of learning and a passion for music fused with his charismatic personality, he was able to convince anyone to follow him to the promised land of understanding and loving classical music. He was able to find a happy medium between purely technical discussions and "the music appreciation racket" (a term coined by Virgil Thompson). By using metaphors familiar to his audiences (e.g. the Lennon-McCartney song "And I Love Her" to demonstrate the sonata form), and comparing classical music to other more familiar styles (folk, jazz, and rock), he became America's most popular and respected music educator by combining enlightenment with entertainment.

Leonard Bernstein, 1955
Credit: Library of Congress

At first, Bernstein didn't think much of television as a medium to carry his message. But when he married the Chilean-born actress, Felicia Montealegre, in 1951, and saw how effective she was in several early TV dramas, he changed his mind. In 1954 he delivered his first *Omnibus* telecast, reproducing the first page of the first movement of Beethoven's Fifth Symphony on the floor, showing how Beethoven arrived at the final version by conducting the Symphony of the Air (formerly the NBC Symphony under conductor Arturo Toscanini) in the composer's initial sketches. In *The Art of Conducting*, Bernstein unravels its mystery by enumerating the skills that make a great maestro. His *Introduction to Modern Music* is a miracle of clarity in understanding the evolution of music in the 20th century—in a mere 49 minutes.

In 1958, two weeks after he was appointed conductor of the New York Philharmonic, he wrote and presented his first Young People's Concert on national television, *What Does Music Mean?* For the next 14 years, he gave a staggering 53 telecasts on a variety of musical subjects, never reluctant to explain difficult musical terms. In *Musical Atoms, A Study of Intervals* (1965), he plays the Beatles song "Help" on the piano to demonstrate the interval of descending seconds—and the viewer sees one kid's face lit up with the joy of discovery. In *What Does Music Mean* (1958), Bernstein divorces the stories, atmosphere and pictures from 'program music,' asserting that it's the emotions and feelings music elicits from the listeners that's the real meaning of the notes. In his 1959 *Humor in Music,* the maestro defines humor as the juxtaposition of clashing incongruities—things that don't make sense together (nonsense). Then he defines different types of humor in music with examples—wit (the last movement of Haydn's 88th Symphony), satire (Prokofiev's *Classical* Symphony), burlesque (Copland's 'Burlesque' from *Music for the Theatre*), among others.

Bernstein wrote all his scripts by hand and a staff of five provided feedback. Even though they could have been taped, they were all done live in Carnegie Hall and Philharmonic Hall. Producer Roger Englander wanted the shows to appear spontaneous, even though they were tightly scripted. He used tight close-ups of soloists and audience members, catching the children's reactions. One letter from an elementary student said, "Please play the tune of *Peter and the Wolf* again. And the next time, use your baton!" Technical rehearsals started at 6am the morning of the show; the orchestra rehearsed at 8am; there was a dress rehearsal at 10am and the program aired at 11am. By 1960, 90% of the population had television sets, so Bernstein reached millions of Americans. He featured young performers (Lynn Harrell, André Watts), composers (Aaron Copland, Gunther Schuller), and conductors (Edo de Waart, Seiji Ozawa, Claudio Abbado). He did complete shows on Stravinsky, Mahler, Hindemith, Sibelius, Shostakovich and Ives. The Young People's Concerts won nine Emmy Awards in a ten-year period. They were so popular with adults that they were telecast for three years at 7:30 on Sunday evening. But Bernstein's educational influence went beyond television.

HIS TEACHING LEGACY

Perhaps Bernstein's most important teaching legacy is the influence he had on American conductors, who now hold leadership positions with American orchestras. Michael Morgan, conductor of the Oakland-East Bay Symphony, comments that Bernstein inspired and trained American conductors to perform many kinds of music—jazz, contemporary music, popular music—as well as making a commitment to program young people's concerts. American Kent Nagano, former Music Director of the Berkeley Symphony and now Music Director of the Bavarian State Opera and the Montreal Symphony, relates an incident where he went to Bernstein's apartment for a conducting lesson. They discussed a-bar-and-a-half chord progression of a Tchaikovsky symphony for an hour. "In that session I learned what kind of a responsibility it was to call yourself a conductor," Nagano stated.

One of Bernstein's prize pupils was Marin Alsop, the Music Director of the Baltimore Symphony Orchestra. She remembered that his respect for the music was grounded in a continual quest for imagining what the composer's intention was by relentlessly studying the score. "Every musician respected him," she said, "he'd come to a concert and say, 'I've conducted this score hundreds of times, and I've been wrong all these years,' before he started the rehearsal." Jazz musician Dizzy Gillespie once wrote a letter to Bernstein saying, "Looking at you on Channel 2, I just discovered that the beat is not in the wave (of your arms), but in the jerk of the wrist. Much love, Dizzy."

Another part of his teaching legacy was his belief and defense of tonality in the midst of the mid-century academic embrace of atonality, as created by Arnold Schoenberg's serial (12 tone) compositional technique. In 1971, avant garde composer George Rochberg had shocked the musical world by writing his *String Quartet No. 3* in a neo-Romantic style. Bernstein sensed an opportunity to champion tonality, and in the fall of 1972, he was appointed Charles Eliot Norton Professor of Poetry at Harvard University for a year. He lived on campus, counseled students and gave six multimedia lectures, using live musical examples which he performed and conducted. They were eventually taped for television.

He employed Noam Chomsky's linguistic theories in an attempt to prove that there were "analogies between linguist universals and the natural music universals that arise out of the tonal harmonic series." But Bernstein's analogy lacked the clarity of the comparisons that made his Young People Concerts so lucid.

But when it came to tracing the development of tonality using twentieth century composers as examples, his analysis was brilliant, if biased. In the beginning of Lecture 5, "The Twentieth Century Crisis," Bernstein asserts that, "Tonality is immortal as long as it is continually refreshed and enriched by bigger and better ambiguities, both chromatic and metrical ones." He analyzed, played and conducted the music of Schoenberg, Ives (whose composition *The Unanswered Question* was used as the title of the Norton Lectures), Mahler, Stravinsky, and others to support his defense of tonality. The question Bernstein asserts is "Whither music in the Twentieth Century?" He uses Berg's Violin Concerto to demonstrate the use of serialism that sounds tonal. "See, he argues, music can sound tonal, even when it's not!" Later, he said in a 1989 interview with Jonathan Cott, "The point is that there shouldn't be a law against any kind of music. Serial music can be written and there's no reason why it shouldn't be. And twelve-tone music is great, and Dadaism is great, and all kinds of music are great, but not at the expense of tonality, which constitutes the root of music." The wide variety of music that composers write today—tonal, atonal, multicultural, etc.—is a testament to the courage of Bernstein's convictions that helped to free composers to write from their heart, regardless of the loss of respect from their peers.

Bernstein's own compositions explore the musical crisis of the twentieth century. It's the very existence of those conflicts and their resolution that makes his music memorable and relevant today.

THE COMPOSER

Leonard Bernstein's compositions reflect the struggles to define his identity as the face of classical music in America. Famous as a conductor, educator, man about town, Broadway and classical composer, his time was divided between many talents. His flamboyant extroverted persona loved influencing and working with people—whether they were musicians of the New York Philharmonic, the kids under his spell at the Young People's Concerts, or composers hungry for feedback from the maestro. Composing serious works was an isolated activity, harder to fit into his busy life. He took leaves of absence from conducting to focus on writing, but those works rarely rose to the brilliance of his musical collaborations—*West Side Story, Candide, Mass*, etc. The one exception was *Chichester Psalms*, a gloriously tonal work written in 1965 while on a sabbatical. Although haunted by the belief that he never penned the "great American symphony," some of his works are loved and performed often today. Others deserve to be, but have been forgotten.

As with Gustav Mahler, Bernstein was torn between two worlds—Jewish and Christian, composer and conductor, tonality and atonality, popular and classical. As we have seen, as a composer and conductor, Bernstein disagreed with his professional colleagues, who were smitten with 12-tone composition. In his Norton Lectures, he posited that Mahler's *Ninth Symphony* summed up the end of tonality and the great arc of Austro-Germanic music that started with Haydn and Mozart. At the same time, that symphony opened the door to the atonality that Schoenberg and others ushered into the twentieth century. From Bernstein's perspective in 1973, it was unclear whether one or the other would become the dominant style in music. As we shall see, his late compositions integrated tonality and atonality, but emerged sounding tonal. We now know that the distinction between the two styles has vanished, fused together by the influences of other musical cultures and the infinite variety of American musical creativity—popular, classical, jazz, rock, minimalism, Broadway, etc. Bernstein's compositions visited a plethora of styles in American music, and that's one of his legacies.

Bernstein continued and extended the legitimization and acceptance of integrating the popular music of his American culture with the legacy of European art music. He grew up with the sounds of Gershwin and Jerome Kern, played jazz piano in nightclubs, and as a teenager organized summer productions of Gilbert and Sullivan in his home. His gregarious personality made him a born dramatist, so it's no wonder that there was a theatrical element that pervaded his compositions. He produced a drag version of Bizet's *Carmen* at age 16, singing the lead role and playing the piano. At Harvard, he chose to study classical music and was influenced by Copland (who became his mentor and colleague), Hindemith and Stravinsky. Even in his brief but brilliant foray into composing Broadway musicals, he never forgot his classical training. *West Side Story* was the first Broadway musical to be scored for a symphony orchestra. His *Mass* is a work that summarizes American music of all genres when it was composed in 1971. Would the compositions of John Adams be as eclectic without Bernstein's boldness in mixing musical styles and calling them "classical?"

Leonard Bernstein, 1945
Credit: Library of Congress

THE EARLY WORKS

Bernstein was first noticed as a classical composer in 1942, entering a New England Conservatory of Music competition with his Symphony No. 1 "Jeremiah." Taking the story of Jeremiah, who preached in Jerusalem from 628 to 586 B.C, warning of the city's destruction due to religious corruption, Bernstein constructed a twenty-four minute symphony that's succinct, gripping and very moving. "Prophecy" dramatically warns of the coming doom, a movement emotionally congruent with the events of World War II. "Profanation" is an angular rhythmic scherzo depicting an unscrupulous priest mocking Jeremiah, but there's never a sense of maliciousness. It's almost as if Bernstein is celebrating the urban contentiousness of his beloved New York. "Lamentation," with a mezzo-soprano, is a moving and lyrical statement of loss. It didn't win the competition, but won the New York Music Critic's Circle award. Symphony No. 1

may not be the great American symphony that Bernstein desired, but it's the best of his three symphonies, vastly underrated and an auspicious first major work.

Although his conducting career claimed the limelight in 1943, when he became an overnight sensation in his New York Philharmonic conducting debut, a year later Bernstein collaborated with playwrights Betty Comden and Adolph Green and choreographer Jerome Robbins to write the music for *On the Town*. The premise of three soldiers on leave for a day flirting with women in New York City may be outdated now, but the idea was real in 1944, in the midst of World War II. The music is delightful (reprising music from his 1944 ballet, *Fancy Free*). The show ran for 463 performances and earned the composer $100,000 for five weeks of work. The entertaining 1949 movie of the same name with Gene Kelly and Frank Sinatra rewrote Bernstein's score, so he asked to have his name removed from the credits. The later jazzy musical, *Wonderful Town* (1953), also a Comden-Green collaboration, used a similar premise (two young girls from rural America coming to New York), but the music was different.

Bernstein's attraction to jazz resulted in two works at the end of the 1940's. His Symphony No. 2 "The Age of Anxiety" was based on a poem by British poet W.H. Auden. It was about three men and a girl in a bar engaged in a "symposium on the stages of man," one of many works that framed Bernstein's struggle with the meaning of life. Structured as a piano concerto with a prologue and seven variations, it's jazzy and ends with a beautiful orchestral chorale. *Prelude, Fugue and Riffs* is a short work written for clarinetist Woody Herman that is a sassy essay on the virtues of jazz.

Only Bernstein could have the gall to write an opera about a miserable marriage set in a classic American suburban setting while on his honeymoon—*Trouble in Tahiti*. But the 45-minute piece was more about his past (the husband was named Sam—his father's name) than the prospects for future happiness. Critic Irving Kolodin observed, "Two emptier, duller people never lived; and if they did knock their heads together nothing would result but a muffled thud." But the music satirized marriage and postwar American materialism, which allowed the composer to write a score bursting with energy and rhythmic excitement. The arias "What a Movie" and "There Is a Garden" are classics. Conductor Nicole Paiment, who led a brilliant performance with San Francisco-based Opera Parallele in April, 2013, comments, "In *Tahiti*, Bernstein invokes, with disarming musical ease and accuracy, the values of 1950's society. The integration of popular idioms into a classically woven musical fabric makes the work refreshing and firmly grounded in the American culture of its time." Three decades later the score was expanded into a second opera, *A Quiet Place*, but times had changed and the couple's reconciliation seemed clichéd.

Trouble in Tahiti contained cinematic transitions—fades and cross-cutting—so it was logical that the never-satisfied Bernstein was looking for a movie to score. In 1954 Hollywood beckoned in the form of a gritty black-and-white film based on Budd Schulberg's screenplay about violence and corruption among longshoremen on the docks of New York—*On the Waterfront*. Bernstein was so upset at the way the movie chopped up his score that he wrote a *Symphonic Suite* from the film. Listening to the score brings back vivid memories of this incendiary movie—the solo horn beginning that mirrors the empty milieu of the waterfront culture—the timpani and sax that portray the violence of the docks—the tender love theme between Terry (Marlon Brando) and Edie (Eva Marie Saint)—the slashing horns and timpani that describe the bloody fistfight between Terry and Johnny Friendly (Lee J. Cobb), and the moving climax as Terry leads his colleagues back to work. The movie won eight Oscars, but none for the music score. It was the composer's only film score, and the suite is a perfect evocation of the movie's drama, milieu and powerful emotional impact.

About the same time Bernstein began to collaborate with playwright Lillian Hellman on an operetta/Broadway musical that updated Voltaire's 1759 novella, *Candide*. It satirized optimism, the best of all possible worlds, in the face of its characters' many personal disasters. Hellman wrote a serious libretto meant to protest the anti-Communist Congressional investigating committee that persecuted her and many other artists and writers. Bernstein wrote a delightful score that made subtle fun of European opera. *Candide* opened on Broadway in 1956, but the music and words never meshed and its episodic nature lacked a cohesive and dramatic plot. It closed after only 73 performances. But a revised 1974 adaptation ran for 700 performances and Bernstein recorded it in 1989. Forget about the convoluted plot, with characters dying and reappearing, but relish the captivating score. The tuneful, rollicking overture is pure optimism and performed often. In "The Best of All Possible Worlds," Bernstein's bouncy music delightfully convinces the listener that war and snakes are a good thing. Candide's meditation "It Must Be So" and "Candide's Lament" are touching tributes to lost love. "I Am Easily Assimilated" (Old Lady's Tango) is a saucy number as sung by the great Christa Ludwig in Bernstein's recording. "The Ballad of Eldorado" is a lovely ode to choosing love over gold. "What's the Use" is a delightful aria mocking corrupt casinos. "Nothing More Than This" is a gorgeous lament for love that appears to be lost. The final number, "Make Our Garden Grow," is one of the great American songs/arias of the twentieth century: a glorious hymn to love's acceptance and commitment. As good as *Candide* is, Bernstein's best was yet to come.

WEST SIDE STORY

One day Bernstein took the wrong exit off the Henry Hudson Parkway and ended up under a huge causeway by the river on 125th street. "All around me Puerto Rican kids were playing, with those typical New York City shouts and the New York raucousness. And yet, the causeway backdrop was in a classic key, pillars and Roman arches. It really contains the theme of *West Side Story*," Bernstein remembers. The clash of cultures, love conquering prejudice, tradition challenging progress, and youth versus maturity, are some of the themes that stamp *West Side Story* as the classic American setting of Shakespeare's *Romeo and Juliet*.

Choreographer Jerome Robbins approached Bernstein in 1949 with the idea of a modern *Romeo and Juliet*. At the time Bernstein was busy developing his conducting career and was influenced by his mentor Koussevitzky, who disdained musical theater. The matter was dropped until 1955 when Robbins again proposed the idea. Arthur Laurents was the playwright, author of *Home of the Brave*, a play depicting the reactions to war of an ethnically diverse group of soldiers; it was a drama that moved Bernstein. Laurents chose the 27-year-old Steven Sondheim as the lyricist. Although Sondheim was more interested in writing his own shows, his mentor Oscar

Hammerstein II convinced him to do it. The extroverted Bernstein had written some lyrics, but the slower-working, introverted Sondheim found them too sweet. Sondheim wanted gritty realism that straddled the line between reality and art. The two men worked out their differences and at the end Bernstein acknowledged Sondheim's contribution by giving him full credit as lyricist.

The fabled artistic team of Bernstein, Laurents, Sondheim and Robbins had their differences, but ultimately established a process that worked. Meryl Secrest's biography, *Leonard Bernstein: A Life*, describes it vividly. Laurents would conceptually shape the story before writing the dialogue. "Steve [Sondheim] had to take dictation and character from the playwright; then he and Lenny would work on the songs. As for Jerry Robbins,...[he] would want to know what the dance was about, so I would write him a scenario," Laurents described. "All three of them fought me on 'Gee, Officer Krupke,' but I sold it to them by arguing that the song was the equivalent of the clowns in Shakespeare," he asserted.

In Jonathan Cott's entertaining book, *Dinner with Lenny*, Bernstein describes how hard it was to cast *West Side Story*— "...the actors had to be able to sing *and* dance *and* be taken for teenagers. So we settled on a mixture—some were actual teenagers, some were twenty-one years old, some were thirty but *looked* sixteen." Jerome Robbins, who conceived, directed and choreographed the play, was a perfectionist who made incredible demands on the cast. Carol Lawrence, who played Maria, would be demolished by Jerry's demands and Lenny would put his arms around her, and say, "come on, let's do the balcony scene. I'll play it for you." Even Bernstein would back down from confrontations with Robbins.

Financed by Roger Stevens and Harold Prince, and Robert E. Griffith, *West Side Story* opened in September of 1957. It ran for 732 performances on Broadway and the recording of the cast album sold a million copies. The movie, made in 1961, won ten Academy Awards and Best Picture. It became a staple for high school and regional theater productions.

The insightful Alex Ross in *The Rest Is Noise* identifies the genius in *West Side Story*. It is "a beautifully engineered piece of pop theater, fueled by bebop melody, Latin rhythm, and old-school Tin Pan Alley lyric craft. It is also a sophisticated essay in twentieth-century style." He goes on to analyze the intervals used by Bernstein and Schoenberg, "emblematic of eternal striving and conflict." *"Maria"* became a popular hit, yet it's the resolution of the dissonance in the melodic line that makes it so pleasing. The rhythmic scoring was inventive, especially as heard in the composer's arrangement of the *Symphonic Dances*. The finger snaps in the score have remained a cultural signifier for rhythmic movement. It was the first time a musical was scored for a symphony. The songs that Bernstein wrote had enough musical integrity to easily be transferred to many arrangements—jazz pianist Marian McPartland made an album of its music.

In June of 2013, Michael Tilson Thomas and the San Francisco Symphony gave the first concert performance of the complete Broadway score of *West Side Story*. The combination of a small, (about 35 members) first-rate symphony performing Bernstein's score, as orchestrated by Sid Ramin and Irving Kostal, and superb Broadway/operatic voices revealed the work to be a *modern* masterpiece, and maybe the first real Broadway opera, although *Porgy and Bess* would compete for top honors. "The Dance at the Gym" and the "Ballet Sequence" in the second act are rhythmically complex, dramatically compelling and emotionally riveting. Fortunately, the performance was recorded and will be available in the spring of 2014.

West Side Story made Leonard Bernstein famous, but it also blurred his identity: was he a classical composer or a show music composer; was he a conductor or a composer? One aspect of Bernstein's musical genius is merging popular and contemporary musical styles.

MASS

Barely a year after the success of *West Side Story*, Bernstein was appointed Music Director of the New York Philharmonic, and for over a decade his attention turned to classical music—conducting, recording and delivering the televised Young People's Concerts. When he left the New York Philharmonic in 1968, Jacqueline Onassis-Kennedy commissioned Bernstein to write a Mass in commemoration of her late husband and the opening of the Kennedy

Center. He worked on it for three years—with unlimited funds—and collaborated with lyricist Stephen Schwartz to compose what turned out to be the ultimate summation of Bernstein's diverse musical powers: a liturgy of opposites. It's based on the structure of the traditional Catholic liturgy, but Bernstein injects parts of Jewish liturgy and some Jewish music into the score. It combines classical music (shades of Stravinsky, Orff and more) with Broadway influences (*Godspell* and *Hair*). It contains rock music, gospel music, the blues, Hebrew chants, operatic arias, and Broadway songs. Formally called *Mass, A Theatre Piece for Singers, Players, and Dancers*, it employs 200 performers—a children's choir, soloists, a rock combo, street singers, altar servers, marching bands, a full symphony orchestra and the Alvin Ailey Dance Troupe.

The theme was Bernstein's life story: the loss of faith. "It was a story piece about conflict and resolution, tied into a complete package. It was Leonard Bernstein's Mahler's *Eighth Symphony* (called the *Symphony of a Thousand*)," said conductor Marin Alsop. The furor of the Vietnam War was at its peak, and this was Bernstein's protest oratorio. The story was of a contemporary young male celebrant, dressed in jeans with an electric guitar, who celebrates God and then journeys through doubt, anger (hurling the sacraments on the floor in a fit of rage), and finally affirming his faith. Bernstein's collaborators begged him to cut the length of the 100-minute work, and he agreed to some cuts for the preview. But nobody could convince him. "Now you've all had your fun. Everything goes back tomorrow," he demanded.

Leonard Bernstein in rehearsal for *Mass*, 1971
Credit: Library of Congress

At the 1971 opening, when Bernstein ended the work by stating the traditional benediction "Go in Peace," the audience sat silent for three minutes, and then erupted into wild applause. Rose Kennedy (JFK's mother), a devout Catholic, sat stunned at the composer's brazen dissection of the traditional liturgy. Bernstein cried, and a reporter commented that "The handful of men who'd lingered at the VIP reception stiffened..." The work was a popular success, especially with the young, selling over 200,000 albums, and productions ensued in Los Angeles and Cincinnati. But *The Catholic Standard* called it a "perversion of the liturgical act" and "a sacrilege." Critics were divided. Paul Hume called it "the greatest music Bernstein has ever written," but John Simon said it was "derivative and attitudinizing drivel."

Listening to *Mass* more than forty years after its premiere, it is easy to accept the diversity of musical styles and the eclectic combination of the formal Latin mass and the hip language that Steven Schwartz wrote. His libretto has some gems: the rock singer's words of doubt: "What I say I don't feel. What I feel I don't show. What I show isn't real. What is real, Lord, I don't know." Paul Simon's trope in the Gloria: "Half the people are stoned. The other half are waiting for the next election" is now famous, and still relevant. Some will cringe at the rock and blues singers' lyrics. Stephen Sondheim criticized the libretto, saying to the composer, "Have you ever thought of translating it into Latin?...So you won't have to listen to the words."

There are great musical moments: "A Simple Song" is one of the composer's best. There's an innocent joy to the "Kyrie Eleison." "The First Orchestral Meditation" brilliantly creates a mood of doubt and anger. "The Lord's Prayer" and the "Sanctus" are stunningly beautiful. Perhaps some of the rock segments have lost their shock value, but the lyrical moments still touch the heart.

The *Mass* lacks the dramatic coherence of *West Side Story*. The Celebrant's plunge into the angry rant (his disbelief in God) that leads to the desecration of the altar seems motivated by Bernstein's love for the dramatic. What's missing is the Celebrant's internal motivation. Of course, the Celebrant is really Bernstein himself, and it was a period of angry outbursts against the Vietnam War. The listener is left to look for a simple song within for hope and belief in God. *Mass* is still a walk on the wild side of Leonard Bernstein, endlessly fascinating and a memento of its time. Yet, there also is a wistful sadness that predicts Bernstein's later years.

LATE MASTERPIECES

Bernstein's wife, Felicia, had tolerated his multiple affairs with men, but when she found him in bed with Tom Cothran in 1976, it was a situation that really threatened their marriage of 25 years. Although their reconciliation indicated their very real love for each other, Felicia was sick with cancer and died on June 16, 1978. It was a dark time in Bernstein's life, exacerbated by continual smoking and heavy drinking. Nevertheless, he continued conducting and composing.

His third and last ballet for Jerome Robbins was *Dybbuk* (1974), written for the 25th anniversary of the establishment of Israel. Two men promise that their son and daughter will marry each other. The girl's father breaks the promise, and the boy seeks power from the Kabbalah to force her to marry him. But satanic forces (Dybbuk) destroy him, his disembodied spirit possesses the girl, and she joins him by destroying herself. The conflict between good and evil is represented by tonal and atonal music, but the differences are hard to identify, so seamless is the transition between one and the other. The ballet was not performed often, but it's a dark and powerful score. The integration of the two styles seemed to alienate both tonal and atonal believers. The relative difficulty of the music in *Dybbuk* has obscured a masterpiece. It's worth the time to hear and understand this score, especially part 2 and part 3 of the music that Bernstein arranged into two suites.

Songfest is a cycle for six singers written for the American bicentennial in 1976, but delivered late. Bernstein celebrates America's diversity by choosing a variety of poems penned by well-known authors—Frank O'Hara, Lawrence Ferlinghetti, Walt Whitman, Langston Hughes, Gertrude Stein, Edgar Allan Poe, among others. The music and subjects represent the heterogeneity of the American landscape. They include a grand and moving sextet—a parody of patriotic hymns; a sexy Latin female rant on immigrant independence more radical than Anita's satirical "America" in *West Side Story*; a heartbreaking dirge to forbidden homosexual love; a powerful bluesy outcry at racial discrimination; a wry, tongue-in-cheek frolic; and a serious Mahlerian ode to lost love. The 12 songs represent Bernstein at his most imaginative and eclectic.

Bernstein's last major work, *Arias and Barcarolles* (1988) is an affectionate musical comment on the ups and downs of conjugal love—a topic familiar to the composer. In 1960, Bernstein had played a concert of Mozart and Gershwin at the White House, and President Eisenhower greeted him, saying, "You know, I liked that last piece you played; it's got a theme. I like music with a theme, not all those arias and barcarolles." The comment, which awkwardly fell on the musically sophisticated Bernstein, stuck with him. Bernstein resolves the tonality-atonality conflict by integrating both into different musical styles that are memorable. The vignettes include a bedtime story that Bernstein's mother told him about a lost rabbit with a humorous reference to Mahlerian angst; a dark and whimsical reflection on lost love; a beautiful song that echoes the wonderment of the birth of his son Alexander; the young composer's memory of a Jewish wedding where an itinerant violinist performs with vitality and emotion, and a warm and wacky tribute to the family of Charles Webb, the Dean of the Indiana University School of Music. It is a sunny, witty and intimate work that's a welcome reprise from the angst of his later years.

LAST YEARS

Especially in his last years Bernstein indiscriminately indulged in public behavior that proved embarrassing to his friends and tarnished his legacy. His guilt around the breakup and loss of Felicia clashed with his overt homosexual desires and behaviors. Mentoring sessions with young male musicians became momentous learning experiences for them, but they worried about possible sexual invitations from the Maestro. Bernstein was lonely and sought solace in medication—prodigious amounts of alcohol, Lithium for depression and Halcion for insomnia. "God knows I should be dead by now. I've been smoking forever; I drink; I stay up all night; I'm overcommitted everywhere," he admitted in 1988.

But his musical triumphs continued. In an all-Copland concert in 1989, the two American giants embraced, and critic Tim Page enthused, "the wunderkind has become the grand old man." The fall of the Berlin Wall and the unification of Germany created a worldwide performance opportunity in Berlin. Bernstein conducted

Beethoven's 9th Symphony at midnight on Saturday December 23, 1989, when West Germans were first allowed to cross the border without visas. The whole cast had a bad case of the flu, and an exhausted Bernstein had just returned from a recording session of *Candide* in London. Substituting "freedom" (*Freiheit*) for Beethoven's original "Joy" (*Freude*), in the final movement, Bernstein was in his element, but he returned to America hardly able to stand.

In April of 1990, Bernstein found out that he had mesothelioma, a virulent form of cancer in his left lung, and he knew he was dying. But he made one last trip to his beloved Tanglewood in the summer of 1990. Although he could hardly stand, he was scheduled to conduct Copland's Third Symphony with the student Tanglewood Music Center Orchestra. It took an eight-hour rehearsal with that orchestra to whip them into shape, but critic Richard Dyer called it "a great performance, much better than his last concert," a couple of days later.

That concert, with the Boston Symphony Orchestra, on Sunday August 19, 1990, included a performance of the Four Sea Interludes from Britten's opera, *Peter Grimes*, Bright Sheng's orchestral setting of *Arias and Barcarolles*—conducted by Carl St. Clair—and Bernstein's last public appearance—a performance of Beethoven's Seventh Symphony. It was an event few could forget, punctuated by a moment in the third movement when Bernstein stopped conducting, and leaned back on the podium in a fit of coughing. The orchestra played on, with cues from Bernstein's nodding head.

On Sunday October 14, 1990, he was in his Dakota apartment, clutched his chest, muttered, "What is this?" and died of a heart attack at age 72. I remember hearing the news in my car on the way back from visiting a friend, and, like everyone else, couldn't believe that Leonard Bernstein was gone.

On the drive to Greenwood cemetery in Brooklyn where his body was interred next to his wife Felicia, the cortege of black limousines passed a large construction site. The workers were lined up, took off their hard hats, and waved goodbye. Buried with Leonard Bernstein was a baton, a score of Mahler's 5th Symphony and a copy of *Alice in Wonderland* (placed there by his family).

AMERICA'S MUSICAL HERO

Through his powerful and charismatic personality, Leonard Bernstein conducted, composed, performed, taught and communicated the relevance of classical music to Americans for five decades in the twentieth century, without mitigating its complexity. That achievement was nothing less than heroic. For me, Bernstein exemplified everything exciting and meaningful about classical music. His recordings of Mahler's Second Symphony and Nielsen's Third Symphony (New York Philharmonic) started my love affair with these composers. When I heard Bernstein's recording of Charles Ives' Second Symphony, the world of American classical music became ripe for exploration. The one time I heard Bernstein conduct—(Mahler's Fourth Symphony and Ives' Second Symphony)—was an unforgettable moment. His enthusiasm and passion for classical music ignited and expanded my own.

It was his self-perceived weakness—spreading himself too thin as a conductor, composer, recording artist, teacher—that was his strength. There were composers, conductors, critics and musicians who were jealous of his success—it was hard to earn a living in classical music then, as it is now. There were critics who blanched at Bernstein's passionate mannerisms on the podium and emotionally overindulgent interpretations. And, especially later in life, his personal behaviors concerned his family and friends. But those musicians who knew him well were amazed at his extensive knowledge of music, literature, and philosophy. Those he mentored—even for a few hours—were profoundly changed by his musical insights. His many recordings attest to his passionate interpretative powers. Anyone who watches his Omnibus or Young People's Concerts telecasts will realize that the mix of clarity, brevity and entertainment are timeless.

Twenty-three years after his death, his musical output remains undervalued and under performed, not only because of its content and emotional generosity, but because of his advocacy for the types of music he composed and conducted. Although some credit must go to Gershwin and Copland for beginning to compose in the American vernacular, it was Bernstein who opened the door for composers to use every kind of music in their "serious" compositions. Perhaps that's his single biggest contribution to the eclecticism that makes contemporary music so vibrant and fascinating. Although his defense of tonality was brave for his time, the distinction between tonal and atonal has become irrelevant today, as both are part of the incredible variety of styles available to contemporary composers.

Bernstein's political activities and viewpoints are often ignored or derided. But he was a true populist who believed that America's diversity was a strength, not a weakness. The music composed today reflects the diversity of not only America, but the world. When you are tired of hearing the endless arguing that magnifies the social, political and economic disparities that is characteristic of America today, listen to the music of Copland, Gershwin and Bernstein. Exult in their music that *celebrates* America's differences. John Adams, the most popular living composer, whose music reflects American culture today, said it best, "I can't imagine my life as a musician without Leonard Bernstein having been there..." As a lover of classical music, I can't imagine my life without Leonard Bernstein, or for that matter, Aaron Copland and George Gershwin.

RECOMMENDED CDS, DVDS AND BOOKS

AARON COPLAND

COPLAND: THE ESSENCE OF AMERICA. Copland the Modernist: Concerto for Piano and Orchestra—*Orchestral Variations—Short Symphony* (Symphony No. 2)—-*Symphonic Ode*. Copland the Populist: *Billy the Kid—Appalachian Spring— Rodeo*. On Aaron Copland: The Man and His Music by Michael Tilson Thomas—*Fanfare for the Common Man*. Garrick Ohlssohn, piano—San Francisco Symphony/Michael Tilson Thomas. 3CDs. RCA 09026-68541-2 – 063511-2 – RCDJ 63719-2.
No living conductor is better able to conduct and articulate the greatness of Aaron Copland than Michael Tilson Thomas, who enjoyed a close relationship with the composer. This three CD set is an easy and inexpensive way to hear essential Copland and MTT's personal experiences with the composer.

A COPLAND CELEBRATION: Volume 1—*Appalachian Spring* (original chamber version), and other works—Columbia Chamber Orchestra/Copland. Sony 89323-4
There are at least five different versions of *Appalachian Spring*, including the original chamber version for 13 instruments and the

better-known orchestral versions (full ballet score and suite). "I have come to think that the original instrumentation has a clarity and is closer to the original concept than the more opulent orchestral version," Copland commented. In a work whose warmth and intimacy is paramount, the chamber version is not to be missed.

COPLAND: *Appalachian Spring* Suite for 13 instruments—*Music for Theatre—El Salon Mexico* (for piano)—Ballads for Violin and Piano—Elegies for Violin and Piano—Two Ballads for Violin and Piano—Harmonie Ensemble New York/Richman—Bridge 9145
Music for Theater and the chamber version of *Appalachian Spring* receives a modernist interpretation in this excellent CD.

COPLAND: *American Songs—Old American Songs* (orchestral version)—*Eight Poems of Emily Dickinson—Billy the Kid* (excerpts)—Dawn Upshaw—Thomas Hampson—Saint Paul Chamber Orchestra/Wolff—Teldec 9031-77310-2

COPLAND: Symphony No. 3—Symphony for Organ and Orchestra—New York Philharmonic/Bernstein—Sony SMK 63155

COPLAND—Music for Films—St. Louis Symphony Orchestra/Slatkin—RCA 09026-61699-2

RICHARD STOLTZMAN: THE ESSENTIAL CLARINET. COPLAND: Clarinet Concerto—CORLIGLIANO: Clarinet Concerto—BERNSTEIN: Prelude, Fugue and Riffs—STRAVINSKY: Ebony Concerto—London Symphony Orchestra/Lawrence Leighton Smith

COPLAND AND THE AMERICAN SOUND: KEEPING SCORE—A DVD created by Michael Tilson Thomas and the San Francisco Symphony.
An excellent film tracing the life and impact of Aaron Copland and his music.

COPLAND: MUSIC IN THE 20'S—3 DVDs—Kultur D4760
Copland's 1965 televised (black and white) lectures are educational, full of unusual works and interesting performances, and reveal the honest and sincere personality of the composer. Excellent transfers and sound.

Pollock, Howard. *Aaron Copland: The Life and Work of an Uncommon Man*
Henry Holt and Company, New York, 1999.
A detailed and lengthy biography of Copland.

GEORGE GERSHWIN

GERSHWIN BY GROFE—*Rhapsody in Blue—I Got Rhythm Variations* for Piano and Orchestra—Songs
Lincoln Mayorga, piano—Al Gallordo, clarinet and sax—Harmonie Ensemble/Steven Richman—harmonia mundi HMU 907492
The original jazz band version by the Harmonie Ensemble must be heard to know how stunning the premiere must have been. The clarinet's whooping slide in the beginning really wails (the player is the 93-year-old Al Gallodoro, who was a reedman in the Whiteman Band), the tempo is fast, and there's a lean and sassy vibrancy to the performance.

GERSHWIN—Piano Concerto in F—*Rhapsody in Blue—Cuban Overture*—Jon Nakamatsu, piano—Rochester Philharmonic Orchestra/Jeff Tyzik—harmonia mundi—SACD—HMU 807441
Pianist Jon Nakamatsu plays the uncut, full orchestra version (over two minutes longer), the tempo changes between sections have more contrast, and the "big melody" is richly resplendent, with spectacular 2007 sound.

GERSHWIN—*Rhapsody in Blue*—Concerto in F—*An American in Paris—I Got Rhythm* Variations for Piano and Orchestra—

***Cuban Overture*—Earl Wild, piano—Boston Pops Orchestra/ Arthur Fiedler—RCA 82876-61393-2**

Fiedler's classic versions of *Rhapsody in Blue* and Concerto in F have long been treasured and the 1959 and 1961 sound still delights audiophiles.

GERSHWIN—RHAPSODIES

***Rhapsody in Blue*—Preludes for Piano—"Short Story"—"Violin Piece"—*Second Rhapsody for Orchestra with Piano*—"For Lily Pons"—"Sleepless Night"—"Promenade"**

Michael Tilson Thomas, piano/conductor—Los Angeles Philharmonic—CBS Masterworks Mk 39699

This 1981 set includes the restored original versions of the *Rhapsody in Blue* (for jazz band) paired with Gershwin's original orchestral score of the *Second Rhapsody for Orchestra with Piano*.

GEORGE GERSHWIN—The 100th Birthday Celebration—*An American in Paris*—*Second Rhapsody for Orchestra with Piano*—Concerto in F for Piano and Orchestra—*Catfish Row Suite* with Scenes from Porgy and Bess—San Francisco Symphony/ Michael Tilson Thomas—Michael Tilson Thomas, p.—Garrick Ohlsson, p.—Audra McDonald, soprano—Brian Stokes Mitchell, baritone. RCA 09026-68931

MTT's compilation of Gershwin works prepared with input and advice from Ira Gershwin. The album includes the original orchestral version of the *Second Rhapsody* and MTT's integration of Gershwin's original orchestral suite of the music from *Porgy and Bess* (which Ira Gershwin called *Catfish Row*, to distinguish it from Robert Russell Bennett's suite) with four of the key songs From the work.

GERSHWIN—*Porgy and Bess*—Willard White, Porgy—Leona Mitchell, Bess—McHenry Boatright, Crown—Cleveland Orchestra and Chorus/Lorin Maazel—Decca 475-8663 (complete version with dialogue)—3CDs

The real greatness of *Porgy and Bess* can only be realized by hearing the complete work, and Maazel's groundbreaking 1976 complete version (with libretto), stunningly recorded, interprets the work as an opera.

***GREAT SCENES FROM GERSHWIN'S PORGY AND BESS*—Leontyne Price, soprano—William Warfield, baritone—RCA Victor Chorus and Orchestra/Henderson—RCA 09026-63312-2**
Leontyne Price was born to sing Bess in this 1963 recording.

Pollock, Howard, *George Gershwin: His Life and Work*, University of California Press, Berkeley, and Los Angeles, California, 2006.
A comprehensive biography of George Gershwin.

Rimler, Walter. *George Gershwin: An Intimate Portrait*. University of Illinois Press. 2009
The author's access to the letters of Gershwin's lover Kay Swift offers new insights into Gershwin and his personality.

LEONARD BERNSTEIN

BEETHOVEN: String Quartets, Opp. 131 &135—Vienna Philharmonic Orchestra/Bernstein—DGG 435 779-2

LEONARD BERNSTEIN—REACHING FOR THE NOTE—American Masters, PBS Production—DVD and VHS—117 minutes documentary—WHE71125—1998
This two-hour documentary effectively communicates Bernstein's many-faceted legacy as America's passionate evangelist of classical music.

LEONARD BERNSTEIN—OMNIBUS—"The Art of Conducting"—One of seven Omnibus programs presented on live television between 1954 and 1958—Archive of American Television, 4 DVDs. EIE-DV-6731

LEONARD BERNSTEIN—THE SYMPHONY EDITION—Sym-

phonies by Mahler, Brahms, Beethoven, Schumann, Sibelius, Haydn, Nielsen, Bernstein, Tchaikovsky and many others—New York Philharmonic conducted by Leonard Bernstein—60 CDs—Sony CBS

The highlights of this set are his exciting Mahler symphonies; the "big band" Haydn exudes joy and excitement; his Nielsen pulses with the thrill of discovery; the 1958 live recording of the Shostakovich 5th Symphony in Russia recaptures an historical event; and his Ives Second Symphony is Americana at its best.

LEONARD BERNSTEIN—YOUNG PEOPLES CONCERTS—25 of the 53 Young Peoples Concerts written and delivered by Leonard Bernstein from 1958 to 1972— DVD—Kultur D1503

LEONARD BERNSTEIN—THE UNANSWERED QUESTION—Six Talks at Harvard by Leonard Bernstein (Charles Eliot Norton Lectures). Book or DVD

LEONARD BERNSTEIN—AN AMERICAN LIFE—Narrated by Susan Sarandon—An Eleven Hour Audio Documentary produced by Steve Rowland and written by Larry Abrams—2004, 2005, Steve Rowland/Culture Works, Ltd.

LEONARD BERNSTEIN CONDUCTS BERNSTEIN—19 of Bernstein's orchestra compositions, including Symphonies 1-3, *Prelude, Fugue and Riffs*, Symphonic Dances from *West Side Story*, *Chichester Psalms*, Serenade for Violin and Orchestra, Mass and many others—7 CD—Sony

LEONARD BERNSTEIN—*Trouble in Tahiti*—*Facsimile*—New York Philharmonic/Bernstein—Sony Classical—SMK 60969

LEONARD BERNSTEIN—*Candide*—Jerry Hadley—June Anderson—Adolph Green—Christa Ludwig—Nicolai Gedda—London Symphony Orchestra and Chorus/Bernstein—DGG 449-656

The 1989 "final version" by the composer is gloriously sung by classically and operatically trained voices. For an alternative

Broadway version:

LEONARD BERNSTEIN—*Candide*—(1974 Broadway Revival Cast)—Mark Baker—Maureen Brennan—Lewis J. Stadlen—June Gable—Sony Classical/Columbia Legacy SK 86859

LEONARD BERNSTEIN—*WEST SIDE STORY*—Jose Carreras—Kiri Te Kanawa—Tiatiana Troyanos—Kurt Ollmann—Marilyn Horne—Orchestra and chorus conducted by Leonard Bernstein—DGG289 457 199

LEONARD BERNSTEIN—*WEST SIDE STORY*—Chita Rivera—Carol Lawrence—Larry Kert—Original Broadway cast recording—Columbia 194841

LEONARD BERNSTEIN—*Candide* Overture—Symphonic Dances from *West Side Story*—*On the Waterfront* (Symphonic Suite)—*Fancy Free* Ballet—New York Philharmonic/Bernstein—Columbia

LEONARD BERNSTEIN—MASS—Jubilant Sykes Baritone—Baltimore Symphony Orchestra/Marin Alsop—Naxos 8.559622-23

In Marin Alsop's recording, Jubilant Sykes as the Celebrant sings a range of styles superbly—operatic, gospel, jazz—that makes him authentic.

LEONARD BERNSTEIN—*Dybbuk*—*Fancy Free*—Nashville Symphony Orchestra/Mogrelia—Naxos 8.559280

LEONARD BERNSTEIN—*Songfest*—Serenade for Violin and Orchestra—Gidon Kremer, violin—Israel Philharmonic/National Symphony/Bernstein—DGG 469836

LEONARD BERNSTEIN—*Arias and Barcarolles*—*A Quiet Place:* Suite—"*West Side Story*:" Symphonic Dances—Frederica von Stade—Thomas Hampson—London Symphony Orchestra/Michael Tilson Thomas—DGG 439 926

LEONARD BERNSTEIN: THE SONGBOOK—Selections from *On the Town, West Side Story, Wonderful Town, Trouble in Tahiti, Peter Pan, Mass, Candide*—CBS MK 44760, mono and stereo
A wonderful compilation of Bernstein's greatest songs, many in original versions recorded from 1950 to 1974.

MOZART: Symphonies 25, 29, 35, 36, 38, 39, 40, 41—Vienna Philharmonic—DGG 474-349-2.

SHOSTAKOVICH: Symphony No. 1—Symphony No. 7 *Leningrad*—Chicago Symphony Orchestra/Bernstein—DGG 427-632-2

Cott, Jonathan, *Dinner with Lenny*, Oxford University Press, 2013

Ross, Alex, *The Rest is Noise*, Listening to the Twentieth Century, Farrar, Straus and Giroux, New York, 2007

Secrest, Meryle, *Leonard Bernstein: A Life*, Alfred A. Knopf, New York, 1994

ACKNOWLEDGEMENTS

In July of 2011 I moved to Rossmoor, a retirement community of 9500 people in Walnut Creek, CA, in the San Francisco Bay Area. If it wasn't for the generosity of Maureen O'Rourke, the Editor of Rossmoor's newspaper, the *Rossmoor News*, this book never would have been written. For the past two years I have written a bi-weekly column for that newspaper called "Modern Classical CDs." This book is an expansion of many articles written under the heading "American Masterpieces." I am indebted to the residents of Rossmoor for providing feedback and support for my articles.

Michael Shahani's *City College of San Francisco's* class "American Masterpieces" inspired me to write about Copland, Gershwin and Bernstein. Dianna Ch'an Moriwaki led me to explore the composers of the twentieth century. Jeff Dunn has designed a cover that captures the essence of Copland, Gershwin and Bernstein.

Linda Morgan, Walt Rimler, Steven Lowe, Angela Beeching, Gil French, Marc Hofstader and Arthur Vogelsang have read my manuscript, edited it and offered suggestions on its content. This is a much better book thanks to their input. Throughout this process my girlfriend, Judy Scott, has provided consistent encouragement, friendship and love.

Robert Moon
Fall, 2013

BIOGRAPHY

Robert Moon has been a writer, administrator, record collector, and classical music concert listener for over 50 years. He has been Assistant Manager of the Minnesota Orchestra, Director of the Kansas Arts Commission, Project Manager of *The New England Regional Arts Planning Study* and City Spirit Facilitator for the National Endowment for the Arts. He is co-author of *Full Frequency Stereophonic Sound: A Discography and History of Early London/Decca Stereo Classical Instrumental and Chamber Music Recordings (1956-1963) on Records and Compact Discs* (1991). He has written numerous record reviews for *Audiophile Audition* (www.audaud.com), and articles and interviews about classical music and musicians for *Strings Magazine* and *San Francisco Classical Voice*. He owned his own used record (LP) business, Classical Gems. For the past two years he has written a bi-weekly column, "Modern Classical CDs," for the weekly paper, the *Rossmoor News*. He has Masters degrees in Business Administration (University of Michigan) and Arts Management (University of Wisconsin) and lives in Walnut Creek, California. He can be reached at moon2780@comcast.net.

Made in the USA
Charleston, SC
14 May 2014